My Lookalike at
the Krishna Temple

Winner of the L. E. Phillabaum Poetry Award for 2019

poems

My Lookalike at
the Krishna Temple

Jacqueline Osherow

Louisiana State University Press
Baton Rouge

Published by Louisiana State University Press
Copyright © 2019 by Jacqueline Osherow
All rights reserved
Manufactured in the United States of America
LSU Press Paperback Original
First printing

Designer: Barbara Neely Bourgoyne
Typeface: Whitman
Printer and binder: LSI

Library of Congress Cataloging-in-Publication Data
Names: Osherow, Jacqueline, author.
Title: My lookalike at the Krishna Temple : poems / Jacqueline Osherow.
Description: Baton Rouge : Louisiana State University Press, [2019]
Identifiers: LCCN 2018034729| ISBN 978-0-8071-6944-5 (pbk. : alk. paper) |
    ISBN 978-0-8071-6943-8 (pdf) | ISBN 978-0-8071-6945-2 (epub)
Classification: LCC PS3565.S545 A6 2019 | DDC 811/.54—dc23
LC record available at https://lccn.loc.gov/2018034729

The paper in this book meets the guidelines for permanence and durability of the
Committee on Production Guidelines for Book Longevity of the Council on Library
Resources. ♾

for Magda, Dora, and Mollie
and for Ray

CONTENTS

(SOMETIMES STARS) I

Autobiography with Joseph

*

Sometimes there are
only stars, waiting
to bow down. Sometimes,
there are only fat oxen.
But then, with no warning,
they've thrown you
in a pit, sold you, bound
you in Egyptian jail.
It's dark there, you don't
speak the language.

**

I left this unfinished
forty years ago. What can
I tell you? Nothing changes.
The skies do still (the right
place, the right time) reveal
themselves magnanimous
with stars, but I've yet
to master the syntactic
leaps in the insular
vernacular of darkness.

***

Luckily, every
year in mid July
or so, a fresh
crop of crickets,
keen, intuitive,

with unparalleled
linguistic acumen,
will all at once
noisily arrive
and till their
departure at
the first frost
offer nightly
simultaneous
translations.

****

The darkness, it turns
out, is even more at odds
than we, hourly wavering
from jubilation—eleven
sheaves of wheat down
on their knees—to what
can only be described
as melancholia:

*****

darkness of a copse
of firs, moonless
dark, darkness
of the clouds
eclipsing darkness,
darkness of the sky
before the heralded
arrival or perhaps even
greater darkness after

the departure
of those desperate,
prostrate stars . . .

******

Is there anyone
who *couldn't* tell
this story? Sometimes
darkness, sometimes stars?

Your one good garment—
an indulgence from your distant father—
stolen off your back
and stained with blood?

****

Van Gogh even told it. You don't
believe me? Go to MOMA.
Press through the crowds
taking selfies. Surely, it's no
coincidence that *Starry Night*
contains precisely—count them—
eleven stars. He knew his Bible,
Van Gogh, had studied it for years,
once planned to be a pastor like his father.

****

Perhaps—who knows?—he'd
have been better off with God;
he'd certainly have avoided
swallowing that lead-filled paint

(cadmium yellow, his favorite).
We, however, would be
seriously diminished, have
only cursory experience of
apple orchards in spring, olive
groves, almond blossoms, cypresses,
what crows over a wheat field
can unwittingly accomplish. We'd
have to trust our own deficient eyes.

****

Just as I, without Joseph,
couldn't have begun
to write a poem. Where
would I have found
the fatal wherewithal
without corroboration
from those kneeling
sheaves of wheat,
that makeshift
constellation
kowtowing across
the heavens, its
eleven chosen
emissaries
plummeting
to earth
until they're
extinguished
at my feet?

****

Of course!—how did I miss this?—
they're *shooting* stars:
the bent backs, the prostrate torsos,
the curve of obeisance, genuflection:
the arc of a meteor across a sky
one brief spectacular salaam.
Unless it's the gilt tip of a scepter
straining to anoint you from some vastly
inaccessible and soon to be
dubious beyond, its outsized
visitation impossibly bright,
compelling your, for once, intact attention
on an errand so drastic, so formidable
it holds even ensuing time at bay.
Nonetheless it's very quickly gone.

****

Sometimes there are only stars
waiting to bow down,
only afterwards
(and then for years
and years) a flimsy
harvest of famished corn.

Sonnet for My Backyard Crickets, Two Weeks Gone

Well, crickets, you're gone again
and again I haven't gotten around
to thanking you properly—a habit of mine.
The same thing happened with my ex-husband,
though, at least, in his case, I tried.
(He hung up on me. Soon after, he died
but that's an old story. And long.)
My plan had been to pay my debt in song,
one from me for a thousand or two from you,
each a precisely calibrated hybrid
of lamentation and nightly lullaby.
From the sound of things, it was pretty hard,
whatever let you know just where you'd find me.
I'm so sorry, crickets. I'll miss you. Thank you.

Backyard Meteor

A clear cold night. I'm taking out the trash,
and nod up to Orion, newly back
in his winter hangout—the chunk of sky
above and to the left of my garage—
and suddenly—what? his fly button pops?
a sleek new nickel slips from his pocket?
or a last drop falls as he gives himself a shake,
the cosmos his fleeting jet-black urinal,
the streak between his legs so quickly gone
I'm not sure what I've seen: a meteor?
in a sky so overrun with city light?
(An early Geminid I'll learn much later.)
All those treks I've made to perfect dark
in hopes of glimpsing a shooting star . . .

Usually I'd cling to such a sighting
but this one disappeared in the debris
of the revelation the following morning,
my telephone's instinct for treachery
in retrospect implicit in its ring,
my daughter broken-voiced on the other end:
I have bad news mostly she's sobbing
and soon I've joined her in an uninhabitable world
in which a girl I still see as a twelve-year-old
claiming floor space in my daughter's tiny room
some giggly, seventh-grade sleepover weekend
(though last March they both turned twenty-one)
stops off at a gun store on her way home
and shoots herself to death in her favorite canyon.

I'm not telling this right. Those details came later:
Cheyenne killed herself is what my daughter
managed into the phone, a sentence
I did not, upon first hearing, parse,
each word at best suggestive of a cognate
in a language I'd at one point understood
but in incoherent grammar. *What? What?*
I made her repeat it at least once
as if a repetition might reverse
or at least revise—*attempted?*—what I'd heard.
Then I *had* understood her? *What? What?*
But my memory is pure incomprehension
and part of me's still squawking in that kitchen
like a bird-chirp alarm clock *What? What?*

It was Cheyenne's mother, Emily, who told me details.
I ran over there as soon as I'd hung up
(just a few blocks away; we'd been in carpools);
I found her outside, taking out the trash;
we clutched each other weeping on the street,
then, eventually, went inside, sat down.
I told my little stories about Cheyenne
(I have a quite a few; she'd been a charmer),
then Emily proceeded to recap
her movements of the day before: the rush
once the boyfriend saw the text, spotting the car,
the receipt from the gun store in the front seat,
how the shotgun had been bought within the hour,
how she, knowing where to look, had found her.

The memorial was two weeks later.
There were photographs. Friends played music.
A woman showed up with an enormous pig
from a farm where Cheyenne used to volunteer.
By then my daughter was home (winter break),
grade school, middle school, high school friends were there,
their parents too—many I hadn't seen in years.
We latched onto one another
though we didn't at all know what to say,
by turns chatty, awkward, lucid, vague.
In the middle of the room was a fierce-looking guy,
a boxer—I rightly guessed—from Cheyenne's gym,
weeping into his hands for the whole three hours
in a folding chair much too small for him.

That was in December; now it's spring
and while I do love the morning birdsong,
those hardy violets that showed up weeks ago
with crocuses, an early daffodil,
toughened up by each fresh round of snow,
I'm not ready to leave off my daily ritual
of willing the earth to spin backwards
(*spin backwards, earth*), however futile
to just an hour earlier that day.
Maybe, next time, there'll be waiting periods
or background checks (*earth, spin backwards*),
the gun-store clerk will just send her away.
But all this greenness keeps pressing upwards;
earth only spins a single way

sometimes, in the pathway of a Geminid
like the textbook one I saw the night she died;
I remembered it eventually, prompted
by a telltale swagger over my garage.
And while I'm not one to extort messages
from the intrigues of the stars, I was tempted
to read it as an omen—she had joined them—
except of course that it was heading downward.
For some kinds of anguish, there's no balm,
no recourse, no deliverance, no sign.
But a meteor did flame in my backyard,
so intensely bright, it made Orion
look pale, even sickly, by comparison,
uncertain though it was and quickly gone.

Counting My Losses

One by fire,
four at will
(one who'd hang,
one who'd pull

the plug on his
own ventilator,
one who'd hit
the crowded water

just beneath
the Golden Gate,
one who learned
to operate

a shotgun
bought an hour past),
one too slowly,
one too fast,

two from age
(one broken hip,
one too weak
to wake from sleep),

one who'd slip
(a cliff-side path),
one surgery's
botched aftermath,

one who wept,
one who prayed,
one heart, alas,
ineptly made,

one who moved
a single thumb
(ALS
her conundrum:

brain intact
while body withers),
cancer of course
for all the others.

(CALL TO PRAYER) II

Eremitaggio

I

The Kotzker Rebbe—
beloved, revered—
spent his last
twenty years
in isolation. Waiting
for insight, some say,
mentally ill, some say,
but judging from his
quotations—*as an ape*
mimics a human
so an old man mimics
himself—he was trying
to avoid self-imitation.

He also believed—
perhaps this was
his motivation?—
that the bulk
of our exertions
(did he mean
the day-to-day, or
the working out
of long-term
aspirations?)
sever us from our
authentic selves.

II

I stumbled upon
his story in disbelief
as a child—or
perhaps it was
a different hermit?—
the practice so alien,
unthinkable. I couldn't
bear the thought
of missing anything,
would pore over
photographs
in weekly *LIFE*
magazines,
storing up future
destinations,
undaunted by
all but the most
extreme degrees
of distance:
that one photo (1963?
'64?) in which my
teeming earth
was a disappearing
disc of blue-
white swirls.

Unendurable
the wonders lost
before I could

behold them
—Tenochtitlan,
Troy, Pompeii—
not to mention
(with apologies
for mingling
sacred and
profane) the
missing Holy
Temple in
Jerusalem.

I was inconsolable
when TV news
showed floods
covering what
newsmen called
the birthplace of
the Renaissance:
still more treasure
I would never see.

III

In one story
the Kotzker Rebbe
had a mason
brick him in
(a few loose bricks,
surely—for food?).

Where would a person,
much less a luminary,
a rabbi, find the heart
to refuse all human
contact? To shut out
even disciples
who'd traveled
miles and miles
to seek a word
from him, their
last resort?

IV

Later, there was
Dickinson's
life story. What
could I do, already
in her thrall at
fifteen, but
tearfully pledge
that if this
was what it
took, I too
would shut
myself inside
my room?

V

But the Kotzker Rebbe
not all that is thought
need be said burned
every single one *not all*
that is said need be written
of what legend claims
were many, many
manuscripts
not all that is written
need be published
his so-called quotations
not all that is published
need be read mere hearsay
as far as I can tell.

VI

But I did not
after all find
it necessary
to shut myself
away and began
(luck? diligence?
obstinacy?)
to acquaint
myself with

earth's
consuming
wonders,
enthralled by
none so much
as the mother lode
I'd thought I'd
lost, at ten,
to a flood.

VII

Nearby, in Assisi,
though still
perplexed
by any willed
detachment
from the world,
I dutifully tried
to climb (there was
no bus) the four
kilometers uphill
to the *eremitaggio*
of St. Francis.

Halfway there,
exhausted, I gave
up, headed back,
but newlyweds
from Cosenza

picked me up
on their way down
and, when they
learned I hadn't
made it, turned
around.

I remember them
much better than
the place itself
(a pink stone
church over a cave?),
carried their address
around for years.

VIII

The Kotzker
Rebbe had
no hermitage;
his hideout
adjacent
to the study
hall, where,
on occasion,
according to
one account,
he sometimes,
frighteningly,
appeared.

IX

And what was
his name, the
carpenter monk
(a Benedictine)
at St. Peter's Abbey
in Saskatchewan?
Brother Michael?
Brother Gregory?
I was there last minute
for a writer's colony—
theirs the only
deadline I hadn't
missed. The meals
were terrible but
they grew golden
raspberries. Gregory/
Michael pointed out
the patch, handed
me a bowl. I had
scratches up and down
my arms for weeks.

Such a charming,
funny guy. We used
the word *hip* then.
He was hip. How
had he ended up
a monk? Before

I left, I asked him.
Oh, I was a heroin addict
he said. *I'd be dead*
if I wasn't here.

X

In every account,
the Kotzker Rebbe
is described as
incisively witty—
can a person *be* witty
without listeners?—intolerant
of stupidity, false piety,
perhaps *that's* why he
shut himself away?

XI

And what of the monks
who closed themselves off
in the tiny bare-bones
cells of San Marco,
each one illumined
with an installment
from the life of Christ
by the aptly nicknamed
Beato Angelico?

One of my first "finds"
(I'd heard of Titian,
Raphael) after I came
to live in Florence,
though on my earliest
visits I barely saw
the frescoes in the cells,
bedazzled as I was
by the heart-
transfixing wings
of the announcing
angel atop the stairs.

(Even Nabokov—
at a rare loss
for words—coopts
them for his first
encountered
swallowtail,
inception of a
life as lepidopterist,
but, to my mind,
a swallowtail's
a swallowtail,
the angel
discernibly
an angel.)

Imagine what it might
have been to spend
a lifetime in that place,

paralyzed along with
Mary every time you
took the stairs,
your every action
(waking, washing,
praying, sleeping)
attended by the ravages
(grim, extreme) of
unrelenting holiness.

Did the monks switch off?
Or did each remain
a lifetime in one cell,
the mysteries embedded
in its plaster walls
accruing, unraveling
accruing . . .

XII

The Kotzker Rebbe
fixed *his* eyes
on nothing eyes
can see, San Marco's
frescoes (a desecration
even to dismiss them
while uttering his
venerated name)
in the category best
translated as *idols*.

XIII

And I'm not dismissing
them. How could I?
Too late for me
to shut away
the trappings of
this world. One way
or another they'd
hunt me down,
however camouflaged
or rearranged by
memory's over-
zealous frippery:
a free-floating
hodgepodge of
minute detail
always at my
whimsical disposal:
a sail reflected
in a lake behind
the profile of a duke;
a trumpeter's
inflated cheeks
inflaming troops
to battle; in
a noblewoman's
braid a rope
of pearls . . .

too late for me
to focus on
a single perfect
item—a brocaded
bodice here, a helmet
there— And
what if that's
the one true
way to know it?

XIV

Perhaps this
is what motivated
the Kotzker Rebbe?
the desire to
achieve complete
attention?

XV

Or perhaps,
as I'm beginning
to suspect, I've
been missing
something
all these years
and the cloister

does have
genuine appeal—
if nothing else,
as hedge against
the long-term
wear and tear
of round-the-
clock exposure
to indignities
of every sort,
the exacting
fallout of
humiliation.

XVI

Who can argue
with an antidote
for heroin?
a mode of speech
discernible to
hummingbirds?
a thousand
seven hundred
seventy-five lyric
bull's-eyes in tiny
hand-sewn leaflets
beneath a bed?

XVII

And the Kotzker
Rebbe still
has followers,
or rather, followers
of *his* follower . . .
(before the holocaust:
one hundred thousand)
and who am I,
off-kilter as I am,
to pass judgment
on their vehement
observances, even
if they do insist
on wholesale retreat
from what for lack
of better words
I call the world?

XVIII

But by which
I mean my own
eclectic haul
of indispensable
indulgences,
daily growing
flimsier and flimsier

and each of which,
as my imagined
vantage widens,
loses its formidable
appeal, and even, wider
still, its singularity,
disappearing
with its armory
of flourishes—
a fresco here,
a tabernacle there—
into the invisible
interstices
between what a state-
of-the-art telescope—
ultraviolet?
infrared?—
might just
be able to reveal
as relentlessly
retreating
blue-white swirls.

The Stork in the Heavens, Revisited

Through the bursting
medina's jumbled
alleyways, the local

farmers pull
their donkey
carts, the lion's

share piled
high with mint,
while others

flaunt cherries,
potatoes, carrots
and a belated

one or two glisten
with artichokes,
whose wild cousins

in the open fields
have already
gone to purple

flower. I find them
in the cemetery
near the beauty's grave

(she wouldn't
convert to Islam
for the prince).

It's still well kept,
the Jewish cemetery
of Fez, though

not too many
mourners will
return, and high

above it
—if only
I could crack

their code—
these gliding
black-and-white

inscriptions
circling and circling,
Morocco's storks,

some coasting,
others on
the prowl.

They're *laklak*
in Arabic
for the sounds

they make:
clacking bills
(they have no call),

each cluster
of nests (storks prefer
to nest in packs)

a cheerfully
percussive
ruckus

whether they're
crammed together
on the ancient

walls of Chellah
or balanced one by one
atop the columns

of Volubilis,
their inhabitants
eavesdropping

on Orpheus' lyre
as he beguiles
a neighborhood

menagerie—monkey,
elephant, oryx,
leopard, peacock—

decked out
in opulent
mosaic

or on a multilevel
metal tower
for power lines,

like the one out
the window of my bus
from Meknes:

on every level, an
extended arm, on every
arm, another nest.

O my insatiable
oblivious storks
how you put

our human
triumphs in
perspective,

our habitual
failure to hold
on to things,

each epoch's offering,
state-of-the-art
or rubble,

an occasion
for a colony
of clacking nests.

And I have
to wonder,
here, in the Jewish

cemetery of Fez,
whose handiwork
we're ignoring

in *our* deafening
oblivious
colonies.

Who's out there
trying to decode
our own

equivocal
inscriptions?
From stone hieroglyphs

to ink on parchment
to LED lights
on a screen

through all our interim
contingencies,
my first transcriptions

from those fly-by-night
contraptions for
which I'm sometimes

so nostalgic:
my grandfather's
enormous black

Underwood,
my sleek little
Lettera 32—pages

hardly perfect,
flecked with white-
out, smudged, messy,

but we always
sounded so
supremely

purposeful
clack clack
clack clack

Fez Postcard/Call to Prayer

A jeweler holds a magnet to his silver
to prove its purity (there's no pull)

A seller wraps a package for a buyer
who's never quite assented to the sale

A flash and then another as a weaver
shuttles spun agave silk through wool

and then a blast of sound, a change of air
at once the market's hustle-bustle trivial

Allahu akbar, Allahu akbar
even if business does go on as usual.

The world seems to refine itself, each color
more acute, each syllable, each smell:

the sharp scent of cedar where a carpenter
planes and sands an ornate floral grille

cumin laced with cardamom and coriander
(the spice sellers' stall), rose petal, fennel

or orange blossom just pressed to attar
escaping from a shapely crystal vial

Allahu akbar, Allahu akbar
every vista turns devotional:

the gorgeous rows of vats for dying leather
(for yellow, saffron, for red, poppy flower,

spearmint mixed with indigo for teal)
are bright-robed worshipers who've joined to kneel

in unison and chant *Allahu akbar*
God is great and powerful

as stragglers head to fountains to splash water
on hands and feet and face and then unroll

the mats they keep with them, each a small
but resolutely holy house of prayer.

I too was taught that sanctity is portable
(words can be carried anywhere)

Allahu akbar, Allahu akbar . . .
our God also great and powerful

but no sound punctuates the air
to call us to our three-times-daily ritual

except on Days of Awe, from the shofar.
Here the otherworldly is habitual

if, perhaps, ignored, the atmosphere
never without at least a telltale

smattering of freshly distilled attar
of the unabashedly eternal

as if a vial were always running over
ready to anoint each head with oil.

A flash in the shuttle of a weaver
A glimmer from a distant market stall

Allahu akbar Allahu akbar
even I, failed believer, feel its pull.

My Lookalike at the Krishna Temple

There's a woman who looks just like you in
Nepal Gopal divulges on my ninth
or tenth visit to his restaurant
(quite exotic, for my local strip mall)
not her apparel of course; she wears a sari.
But if she stood beside you, you'd be sisters.
I've seen her many times; she lives perhaps
three kilometers from my home; worships
with my mother in the Krishna Temple.

Is that the tower in my favorite
repeating photo from the electronic
frames around his walls? a golden-studded
brick extravaganza: part chimera,
part Himalaya, part exaggeration
of a pilgrim's rumor of a glimpsed pagoda
for which I've invented, over my kofta
and yellow dal, a convoluted fable
of a woeful Chinese deity in exile
on whom some locals have taken pity

but it could be the very place my look-
alike approaches every morning for
whatever made her mother's mother's mother
chant the selfsame patterings of syllables
she herself still utters every day
always in a different gold-trimmed sari

(yesterday: opal-colored, spangled gold
tomorrow: amethyst with gold-flecked edges

today, a remnant from her mother's dowry:
diaphanous, if threadbare, near-black lapis
on which the temple's oil lamps detect
smatterings of milky white-gold pinpoints:
her mother's legacy a moonless sky
now miserly, now profligate with stars).

For the most part, she's motionless in prayer
but every now and then her bangled arm
performing some involuntary gesture
clinks a sotto voce tambourine.

Gopal cannot quite recall her name—
but among the electronic photos
(Gopal changes them periodically)
a woman does show up with outsized features:
smile all gums and teeth, expansive forehead,
nose a raptor's beak, socketed eyes,
their blackness goaded on by rims of shadow.

There are—I checked—green-eyed people in
Nepal, perhaps even the offspring of the very
same marauders whose vodka-driven
incursions (did Cossacks ever head east?)
reputedly gave me my own green eyes,
my lookalike in fact a distant cousin.

Let's add a yak-wool shawl for every sari,
a half shade deeper than its sari's silk,
swaths of which we'll use for matching slippers.

Let's still each wayward bangle with a jewel
and then move on to anklets, circlets, nose rings
until she's encompassed by a lavishness
exceeded only by its attendant silence
enabling us to make out (Sanskrit
suddenly our native tongue) her prayer's
undying string of sumptuous words:

I know not any other reality
than the lotus-eyed Krishna . . .
looking like a heavy-laden cloud . . .
his lower lip like the ruddy bimba fruit . . .

Can she mean it? No other reality?
Not even the exploding one inside
her head? the harrowing one? the fickle one?
the fractious, dazzling, disappearing one?
Perhaps she could provide a demonstration
of how to live your life in such close quarters,
preferably a blow-by-blow of every
waking minute until I've taken in
its far parameters: divinity
a countenance (complete with *lower lip*)
you could daily gaze upon and live.
You'd even know its instrument (*the flute*),
the fabric of its garment (*yellow silk*).

Perhaps that's why she's so meticulous,
my lookalike, about her daily saris
(yesterday: sapphire with red-gold swirls
tomorrow: mother-of-pearl with bronze-gold

petals, but just this moment, her mother's
wedding dress: in darkness, indigo
but in the light—a skittish onrush
of unremittingly discordant fireflies
reconciled across a crush of stars).

How is it her mind never wanders?
That's all mine does at weekday morning prayers,
where I can barely focus on saying kaddish
for my own father—the reason I'm there
(ritual my single ready ally
in an ongoing, mostly losing, battle
with unprepossessing emptiness).

But I'm lost on this new diminished planet
where now—unless what Gopal says is true—
I'm the last one standing with my face.

And even when I try I'm no good at this;
unconsummated daydreams call my name.
How does she manage it, my lookalike?
though where, exactly, could her mind wander
with only a single known reality?
which, let's be honest, is all she has.
Chances are, she's pawned her bangles, if she
ever had them, wears the same all-purpose
sari (a hand-me-down from Gopal's mother),
cotton shawl, hemp sandals, every day.

And that was nonsense about the Krishna Temple.
Ranji and Srinivas told me all about it

nineteen years ago at Mollie's naming
(they brought her a tiny silver cup
she drank from each Shabbat for years):
We love synagogue! We had no idea!
It's exactly like Hindu Temple:
people talking all the time, walking in,
walking out, greeting all their friends, shaking hands,
not a single one paying attention . . .

Don't tell me my lookalike's in the back,
telling jokes, like me on any given
Shabbat morning, that is, once I've finished
madly cramming to chant the Torah.
I'm a fraud, a hypocrite, a foul-weather
believer, but I'm also superstitious,
hopelessly sentimental and never
waver in devotion to those words,
the more incomprehensible, the better,
especially when I chant them, with no
vowels or punctuation, just an ornate
silver pointer and a scroll. I'll have learned

them all by heart and still they'll stagger me:
God Himself preempting my own voice
to humor Moses with His unnamed Name,
a Name even an atheist could get
behind, though he'd take issue with its source
(a conflagration, a Teflon bramble),
not that pompous, if resonant, *I am*

that I am—that of course is a gross mis-
translation—but the apologetic
(I hear it with a Yiddish inflection),
resigned *I will be what I will be*
which, pretty much, covers everything,
from a blue figure robed in yellow silk
to a smooth-talking hermetic threesome
to my personal soft spot: a deafening
nonnegotiable, abiding silence.

Who's that gray-haired lady who chants the Torah?
the kids at synagogue ask their teacher—
my daughter—who rewards their good behavior
(a rare commodity in Hebrew school)
by entertaining them with imitations.

Who knows? maybe one of them, in a few years
on junior year abroad in Kathmandu
will stop my lookalike as she's walking
down the street, *there's a woman in Salt Lake
City who looks just like you. I worshiped
with her daughter at the Jewish Temple . . .*

If only Gopal could remember her name.
(I've asked him several times; he says
he's had no chance to ask his mother;
are there no telephones in Kathmandu?)
Not only would it secure her existence,
but I could speak to her, call out to her,

stop her before she starts dressing me up
or fabricating cockamamie stories
about my great-grandmothers and me.

Forget it. I'm no use to you. Go home.
If you like, you can visit Gopal's mother
first, then head three kilometers downhill.

There's a hole in the floor beneath the rug
beneath your bed. Uncover it. Ignore its contents
until you find a box carved of sandalwood,
inlaid with lapis lazuli, white topaz,
tourmaline, coral, moonstone, jade.
Inside, wrapped in muslin, is a sari
woven from untraceable silk thread,
each strand colored by a separate hand
with its private rarefaction of the blue
dominion between sapphire and indigo
and braided with a single golden filament.

I have no idea who worked the loom, or
where, or how exactly the disparate fibers
were beguiled into cloth, but afterward
your mother's mother's mother's mother's mother
whiled away her decade-long betrothal
embroidering each breadth of gold and azurite
with still more strands of gold in Kathmandu.
Put it on. Krishna's awaiting you.
And I won't lie, lookalike. I'm waiting too.

(SNAPSHOTS/SEASONS) III

Spring Arrives Late to Salt Lake City

Why so hesitant, spring? What's the problem?
I've never known you quite this shy.
You're like a new girl in junior high,
avoiding the hallways, the lunch room,
strangely oblivious of your own beauty
or perhaps afraid of it, keeping it hidden.
But what's happening? All of a sudden
you're trying prom dresses on all over the city,
absurdly poufy pinks, whites, purple-reds,
yards and yards of crinoline beneath each skirt.
And now you're tearing them up! Exquisite shreds
cover streets, cars, sidewalks, rooftops, grass . . .
You're back to all or nothing, spring. I'm envious.
I aimed to be like that, but I lost heart.

Storm Clouds over Lupines: Villanelle

LAKEVIEW, MONTANA

Which is the mirror, field or sky?
These silver-purple clouds or purple lupines
in endless sagebrush, gray on silver-gray?

And what's that between them? Is that my
reflection? I should move before it rains.
But which is mirror? Is that field or sky

gazing at her likeness, lazily
touching up the purple imperfections
tarnishing her mirror's silver-gray?

Or are they in cahoots? See? they multiply:
reflections of reflections of reflections.
Perhaps they're both mirrors, field and sky

each redoubling the other's sovereignty
across their spectrum's frugal variations:
purple to silver, silver to gray.

What a pity I'm in the way.
But I flatter myself. The clouds and lupines
don't even see me, just field and sky
dissolving silver purple silver gray.

Autumn Ghazal

Snow on the mountains, clear sky, a hint of gold
in a precocious cottonwood, one strand of gold

enough to make a stand of trees acquisitive
until one long unbroken band of gold

upends the hillsides: a brief reprieve
from a grueling season, my fund of gold

wholly depleted, my heart part sieve,
part punching bag. Whatever command of gold

I once thought I possessed (itself tentative)
was surely just imagined. Drained of gold,

I envy the lindens' brash initiative,
the aspens' shimmy, the torrent of gold

cascading down the willows. Each changed leaf
contributes its fresh supplement of gold

to the landscape's subtle but potent sedative—
or is it perhaps a stimulant?—of gold

and the crickets chime in with their recitative,
as if to amplify the sound of gold:

don't grieve, Jackie, don't grieve, Jackie, don't grieve
what's lost is lost, but you've found gold.

Winter Sonnet

Why not take a lesson from these trees?
They don't fault themselves
for stinting the neighborhood of leaves;
they don't even apologize.
Instead, they concentrate on clearing space
for whatever has the wherewithal to thrive.
Perhaps the trick is just to step aside
and keep your eye out for a hint of grace
which—who am I to argue?—could arrive
at any time at all if it has room
with a modicum of luck or fortitude
and alter everything you think you know,
each bare-bones tree a slumbering imperium
of fleeting sunlight on fleeting snow.

Psalm 27 on Newark AirTrain
(mid-December, 4:15 p.m.)

For an instant, I get a too-brief peek
at an enormous psychedelic hot-pink sun
crowding out a fleet of ugly, sleek
steel-and-concrete slabs on the horizon
through the windows on my left. On my right
the glass rectangle of an airport hotel
is an outsized IMAX, all neon coral
with the last of the sun's reflected light.
Whom do I thank? My Delta pilot,
for landing my plane forty minutes early
in this dizzy crossfire of light on light?
Or the trigger-happy showoff on artillery,
fending off the Newark Airport twilight
with fusillades of gold (*my strength, my light*).

Moonrise, Salt Lake City

DECEMBER 26, 2015

It looks, for all the world, like the holy ghost
in an early Renaissance annunciation:
a light-struck, light-emitting dove in flight.
But there's no Mary. No Gabriel. It's night;
the moon's taking a necessary breather,
a bit too out of shape to slither past
this mountain I hadn't seen was here,
its outlines newly visible as wings
(what's showing of the moon itself's the head).
Don't worry, moon; we all lose our bearings.
You don't have to rise. Stay here instead.
I'll spot you; we could both use an ally
and rumor has it disorientation
is the least resistant pathway to what's holy.

Tilia cordata

Here, near the desert, the air's so dry
even the scent of lilac and peony

won't carry very far. And they've been gone
for a good few weeks now. It's the end of June,

the foothills' transitory emerald
now scorched to a stubborn, bleached-out gold,

the mountains incoherent without snow.
The breeze, sporadic at best, unloading cargo

just to stay afloat, quickly abandons
any pretense of carrying a scent. Only the lindens

(a whim of early dreamers on my street)
from some inner surge of altruism, conceit

or pure naiveté, choose just this instant
to loose, en masse, their all-consuming scent.

I could spend its all too brief duration
just sitting on my porch, breathing it in.

My neighbor hates it—says it's too much—
but my Russian housecleaners used to harvest a batch

of the tiny flowers every summer for tea
prized all over Europe as a delicacy:

in French, it's *tilleul,* the very tisane
that, moistening a random madeleine,

inspired Proust's obsession with *Lost Time*.
It's a main ingredient in Sleepytime

and the *tè per i nervi e per insonnia*
I used to drink in Italy. *Tilia cordata*

is the Latin name, both for tree and flower.
In England it's *lime* (Coleridge's *bower*

hardly a *prison*), its unparalleled
heart-shaped leaves the first green to unfold

in spring, in autumn, the last to fall.
But its best feature, of course, is the spell

cast by its fragrance every June.
A pity this often happens when I'm gone

doing the "research" my daughters call a scam
since it usually involves extracting a poem

from some longed-for place or, sometimes, two.
Three years ago, in search of Art Nouveau,

I scoured Barcelona, Nancy, Glasgow,
and a section of Darmstadt called Mathildenhöhe,

once a *Jugendstil* (art nouveau in German) colony.
I'd never before traveled to Germany

and though I loved each *Jugendstil* detail,
was perpetually uneasy, every guttural

a broken razor blade inside my mouth.
I suppose it was inevitable: the birth-

right of a Jew born in 1956
to parents still reeling from the war's aftershocks.

I have no memory
of a time before I'd heard the word *Nazi*—

always sotto voce, in that nervous hiss
my mother reserved for fatal illness

or—on rare occasions—the obscene.
My earliest recollections from a screen:

Old Yeller, Walter Cronkite, *Pinocchio*
and piles of gaunt bodies in a backhoe,

being shoveled—human bodies—into ditches.
I badgered my mother after hearing snatches

of unassimilable whispered conversation
and wouldn't take a shower until I was seven,

worried gas might come out. That's what my mother
had told me: *gas came out instead of water*

when pressed for what those whispers meant.
Needless to say, I thought it was an accident,

that a malfunctioning shower might cause my death.
Even now, I still prefer a bath

though I know the showers themselves were not at fault,
just as—circumambulating Darmstadt,

in search of still more feats of art nouveau—
it's not as if I didn't know

that the people I saw around me were far too young
for incrimination, their German tongue

a way of putting things like any other.
But though I learn quickly, my entire repertoire

was *ein cappuccino bitte* and *danke schön*
and even uttering those sounds felt like treason.

I decided to go to Worms, where the great Rashi
—a rabbinic wonder—had gone to study

in the eleventh century—
a forty-minute train ride away

but, en route to the station, as I imagined
asking for the Jüdisches Museum, I turned around.

In that setting, the two-word phrase
seemed to sum up the whole dread enterprise:

reducing *Jüdisches* to a museum.
I couldn't bear to utter its name,

much less actually to go there
though I owe to Rashi my first glimmer

of the endless acrobatic feats of words,
their mutability, the daredevil speeds

with which they abolish time and distance.
He could find, behind the most straightforward utterance,

an implicit labyrinthine universe
and another behind that. (At issue was Genesis

chapter 27, verse 19:
fourth-grade Hebrew school with Mrs. Gelman.)

I didn't need a Rashi museum; I had his commentary.
What I needed was another history

or at least a place where mine was less conspicuous;
but my train was a day away. I wandered, aimless

till I remembered reading about a *Jugendstil* gate
to the park at the end of town and then forgot

architecture in a stunning crush of green
expansive trees extending on and on,

so thrilling, after years in an arid climate,
like Philly's Fairmount Park—my father's favorite—

where the surrounding city seemed a shrill mistake
at least to a little girl riding piggyback

through the park her father had wandered as a boy.
In Darmstadt, of all places, his fifty-year-old joy

was newly palpable, though I now wondered
if he hadn't in fact felt a bit bewildered

at being in that spot and fully grown,
as I've always felt when I've brought my children

to my old beloved childhood haunts.
Maybe you're more susceptible in strange environments?

How could a German park bring me my father?
But sometimes what's familiar is so familiar

ubiquity becomes its camouflage;
you don't distinguish it, don't acknowledge

its presence where it doesn't quite belong;
I'm not sure when I realized that all along

I'd been breathing in the smell of linden,
more intense than on my street, the very linden

that kept me on my porch for hours dreaming.
And while it's not really that surprising—

isn't Unter den Linden
the most famous thoroughfare in Berlin?—

that a huge German park would smell like linden
on the final afternoon of June,

I—unhinged already—was undone,
as if the trees themselves were in collusion

to throw me off completely. How could this
thoroughly alien, unnerving place

have anything in common with my home?
Was it a sign? If so, from whom?

And what, exactly, was it saying?
Not that it mattered. I wasn't listening.

It was hard enough dealing with the fragrance,
much less good and evil, guilt and innocence,

which I knew—in any case—are not confined
to a single unlucky piece of land.

But the obvious wasn't obvious in that place;
my principles—such as they were—were powerless

in the face of the matter-of-fact harmony
in evidence around me. Shouldn't Germany

be paralyzed by its hideous statistics?
How could any person reconcile such facts

a mere sixty-eight years further on?
Still, it's a lifetime. And we just have one.

That is, if it isn't ripped away from us.
But mine—by the narrow grace

of eleven years and (some time before that)
a shtetl subsistence so inadequate

it sent my four grandparents across an ocean—
is still intact. Surely, its duration

ought to be directed toward what's beautiful,
my linden this very instant casting its spell,

its outspread branches almost at my porch.
And I'm here for once, within the reach

of its thick, evocative perfume,
an all-encompassing amalgam

of itself and every time I've breathed it in:
my daughters babies, or little children

pointing their fingers and exulting *tree*
then *bird*, then *linden*, then *black-capped chickadee*,

my ex-husband my husband and still alive
or me: disoriented, restive

bolstered by a welcome shock of green
until I realize something like this very linden

must have been attendant on atrocity.
Surely, if not in Darmstadt, then in another city

(Warsaw? Paris? Amsterdam? Berlin?)
some of those millions were smelling linden—

given the tree's prevalence, its heavy fragrance—
as they were being herded onto trains?

My daughters have been known to make bets
before dinner parties about how many minutes

will pass before I bring up the holocaust.
(You're an easy target when you're obsessed;

usually, the winning number's about twenty.)
They're merciless, my girls, if extremely funny

and hardly oblivious of horror.
But they really do think I'm in error;

my narrowness and bias inexcusable.
And I'm weirdly proud of their disapproval.

Let's hope their view won't require accommodation;
but if, in time, it does, no doubt, *their* children

will call them on it, as well they should.
Surely it can't be good

to infuse one of earth's loveliest offerings—
a linden tree in June—with human beings

at their very basest. Something's wrong with me.
Not to mention that my reasoning is faulty.

No one in that appalling circumstance
could pay any attention to a fragrance

and even if they did, who's to say
whether it caused—by brutal contrast—agony

or offered, one last time, a tiny balm?
It's so far beyond me. I'm safe at home

breathing in the fragrance from my tree,
an exquisite, if no longer entirely

untroubled or uncomplicated, pleasure.
But doesn't every good thing have its measure

of imperfection lurking in the wings?
The glass we're obliged to break at weddings

to acknowledge the Holy Temple's destruction?
In a world this damaged, this out of proportion,

what remains untouched? Nothing at all.
Still, who can blame me if I stay a while?

It can't last too much longer, this perfume,
but here, just now, my linden tree's in bloom.

(POEMS FROM THE ALHAMBRA) IV

I. Joyful Paradise

Where exactly do I put my eyes?
This airtight synergy of thrill and balm
Surely this is the most joyful paradise

reads a single verse of a single poem
among ten thousand writings on these walls,
inscriptions everywhere, as if the polychrome

extravaganzas of ceramic tiles
weren't sufficiently luxurious
to cast these all-consuming spells.

Surely this is the most joyful paradise
Is the one in heaven, then, inferior?
or merely less determinedly joyous?

Earth does have its own intrinsic pleasure
sharpened, no doubt, by intrinsic pain
but that's not the joy compounded here,

where all earth's valuables—or all those known
when this palace was imagined—reach their climax,
their elements minutely interwoven:

esoteric truths of mathematics,
Quranic and poetic texts become
grand spectacle, visual artifacts

and only after, oracles of wisdom.
Surely this is the most joyful paradise
Even abnegation turns sublime:

the injunction against making a likeness
entices every nuance of geometry
to startle a reflecting pool with its bare face

and multiply its unsuspected beauty:
infinity made manifest, the golden mean,
the seventeen varieties of symmetry

renounce the rigors of computation
(where exactly do I put my eyes?)
and consecrate themselves to the serene.

Surely this is the most joyful paradise
Pomegranate. Rose. Rose. Jasmine.
Cypress. Myrtle. Jasmine. Jasmine. Rose,

their beds triangles around a hexagon
and alternating trapezoids in rows,
an oleander-covered footpath, then a fountain:

a fleet of light-struck parabolas,
nature here ordered but still natural,
order sovereign but in repose

its influence both dizzying and tranquil,
each ingress a distinct apotheosis
with all of shape and color in its thrall

and flourishes of Arabic in lavish praise
of palace, kaliph, the bountiful
indulgences of nature: moon, stars, trees,

their purest words reserved for the All-powerful,
with an invocation so ubiquitous
I can pick it out on every wall

(an amalgam of *w* and *s,*
where two large strokes loom above the whole).
There's no victor but Allah is what it says

in wood, gold, plaster, ceramic, marble
and out into the intervening stillness
that amplifies and penetrates them all

disciplining hosts of multiplicities
to sacrifice their splendor to this full
and joyful—*the most joyful*—paradise.
But where exactly do I put my eyes?

II. Symmetry I

1

At three or
four, I stumbled
on an iridescent
secret (did
I understand
its power? I'm
not sure) how
beauty inheres
(at least in two
dimensions) in
a slim and ever-
shifting equilibrium
between proportion
and accumulation:

2

flat bright
wooden blocks—
each shape
a different
color—insulated
hours of my
childhood,
however I'd
maneuver
them: an airtight
fit, not a thread

of carpet in-
between, as
they supplanted
its impassive beige
with the florid
hocus-pocus
of geometry

3

six blue
diamonds
splayed like
petals of a flower
left just enough
room for six
green triangles,
each of whose
equal sides
equaled in length
each side of
the blue diamond,
the orange square,
the yellow hexagon

I proudly referred
to as an *octagon*
itself equal
in size to
a mirrored pair

of the strange
red shapes
(*isosceles*
trapezoids
I'd call them
in another
decade)
conjoined
at their sole
unequal sides

4

to a young child
the possibilities
were infinite
the outcomes
elaborate and
splendid:

so much more
exalted than
what crayons
might produce
with their
double-crossing
heavy-handed
scrawl

5

each fresh
arrangement
on the living
room carpet
an otherworldly
visitation, the
aggregate wildly
outdistancing
the parts
assembled
by my newly
potent hands.

6

Here at
the Alhambra,
they return
to me—after
more than
fifty years—
flush with
memory's
hyperbolic
splendor

7

and I want
to imagine
the Moorish
ceramicists
as undisputed
masters of
my pattern
blocks: fitting
shape into shape
in seamless
repetition
dumbstruck
by the reach
of their
own hands

8

but theirs
was a schema
so deliberate,
so esoteric
that modern-day
practitioners
of algebra's
group theory

encounter
these designs
with disbelief:

on the walls
of the Alhambra
appear all
known variants
of patterned
symmetry
in two dimensions,

distinctions I
can barely fit
my brain around:
translation symmetry
rotation symmetry,
simple or glide
reflection symmetry

converging
at the whim of
an all-defining
lattice (triangle,
parallelogram,
hexagon) on which
every pattern
must revolve.

9

For me it's an article
of faith (the mathematics
is a bit beyond me)
that the possible
combinations
of configurations
add up to a mystic
seventeen:

the sum
of the days
required
even by
God
to extract
a resting
universe
from chaos

added to
the quantity
of highly
calibrated
instruments
refining
the efforts
of what
otherwise
would be

our inarticulate
and clumsy
hands

10

all the variations
in two dimensions
compounded
and rendered
indivisible
except by
a halcyon
and nonintrusive
but nonetheless
all-pervasive
one

11

(one more
one and we'd
have arrived
at the radiant,
untouchable
eighteen
which, in Hebrew,
spells out life
itself, as well

as ordering
our prayers—
nine of direct
light, nine of
refracted light—
but that's Kabbalah,
we dare not
go there)

12

and to think
that all I see
is beauty

the multiple
patterns
launching
one another
in a cryptic
magisterial
processional

assiduously
nurturing
the unapt eye
to rise to its
luxuriant
occasion

13

and there are fountains—
I must speak of them—
and gardens
and pillars
minutely carved

and poems
in Arabic
inspiriting the walls
permanence belongs to God . . .

the fingers of my maker
wove my fabric
after setting the jewels
in my crown

14

some mathematicians
will tell you it's not clear
that the artisans
knew what they were doing
as if all seventeen
possibilities of symmetry
could show up in a single
palace by accident

they'll tell you there's no
mathematical treatise
describing
the phenomenon
from that time.

15

But isn't the Alhambra
itself the treatise?
its mathematicians
so certain of their proofs
they performed
them with supremely
complex plasterwork
and monumental
batches of laboriously
fashioned tile:
each piece molded, fired,
colored, fired, glazed,
and fired and glazed
and fired again,
as if time were
a limitless
commodity

16

as it was to me
in front of a black-
and-white barrage
alternately riveting
and boring (a grave-
faced man enunciating
clearly, a Russian pounding
tables with a shoe)
my colored blocks
and I devising pattern
after pattern, an ever-
changing continuum
in seventeen varieties
rotating, reflecting, gliding,
red, orange, green,
yellow, blue: each one
commanded by
an unseen fleet
of elegant axioms
and theorems,
true as very few
dictums are true,
detected thousands
of years ago
on a beach
in Alexandria
and feted on
a hilltop
in Granada

17

but initially—who
knows?—perhaps
a momentary fancy
at the instant
when day one
became day two:

a quick formulation
between light
and darkness
and the strata
of a freshly crafted
firmament, whose
insubstantial
fabric had not
yet been disrupted
by the clamor
of the stars and
sun and moon

the earth itself
still enmeshed
in chaos,
its flowers
and grass and animals
as yet unsummoned
by a voice
unaccustomed

to its own
reverberations,
immaculate
permanent
thorough

18

perhaps it too
is astonished
by its reach,
from each new
utterance a full-
fledged marvel
to which another
marvel will accrue,
pattern after pattern
diminishing the chaos,
motionless in a final
glaze of holiness,
immaculate,
intricate and
very, very good:
heavens, earth
and all their retinue

III. Last Ticket of the Day: Return Visit

Who tore the universe asunder?
Or is it only I who am ablaze?
How did I get here? What's this spell I'm under?

My bones are firewood; my eyes are tinder.
Why this compulsion to gaze and gaze
and burn each ceiling, wall and floor asunder?

Tilework and plaster: fire and cinder,
each patterning a maze within a maze
How do I get out? what's this spell I'm under?

Am I plunderer or plunder?
What's the reckoning? the prize?
Why tear height and breadth and width asunder,

unleash sign after sign, wonder on wonder
only to confound and tantalize?
Where can I be? Is this a spell I'm under

or do mazes within mazes hiss *surrender,*
their exits all on fire, their entranceways,
their interlocking spirals buckling under
with me inside them spellbound burnt asunder.

IV. Symmetry II

I really don't know how I'll get out of here
though the guard does approach . . . *Señora . . . it's time*
and by now I know that my prospective detour

via art and math and history and dream
around the Alhambra will prove impassable
despite my state of semi- (complete?) delirium

or perhaps because of it: I was a fool—
not just to think that highly abstruse math
was the stuff of poetry, each minuscule

trajectory of angle, length, and breadth
(p_1, p_2, p_3 . . .) a revelation,
but for thinking I could even catch my breath.

My head is spinning and will always spin
and it's not just from my run-in with group theory.
Even history, once my own discipline

and still a clear obsession, eludes me,
though I'm rarely much outside its purview
since—call it inertia, sentimentality,

indoctrination, culture—the long, long view,
albeit lopsided and paranoid,
is the go-to vantage point of any Jew

with or without the patronage of God.
It's personal for us, a family story;
we know each episode from the inside

with the bare-faced inexactitude of memory:
one part denial, three parts exaggeration.
When my guide ascribes a trove of household luxury

near an eleventh-century foundation
at the southwest edge of the Alhambra's hillside
to the Jewish vizier of Abdul Rachman—

the great poet: Shmuel Hanagid—
a piece of the Alhambra becomes *mine*.
Not that he'd have let the likes of me inside

but he can't keep me out; it's barely a ruin,
just wildflowers scattered in the grass
waiting for an act of imagination

to conjure up a Hebrew poet's house.
And I can oblige or not because they're *mine*,
my poppies, *my* ranunculus

among so many elements so alien:
mathematics, the Quran, the ubiquitous
appeals to Allah, the Great and Mighty One,

or the Inquisition's edict expelling *us*
signed by Ferdinand and Isabel
in the peerless Sala de Embajadores.

One might have thought they'd choose a cathedral
or some other Christian space for such a purpose
like the eyesore erected smack in the middle

of Cordoba's one-time mosque, so glorious
even the Christians couldn't destroy it all.
But to sign such an edict in the Moors' own palace

seems excessively, vindictively cruel.
On the other hand, when it comes to stamina,
their victims' work and not theirs would prevail.

Spain's greatest monument is the Alhambra
and no one cares much about Charles the Fifth's
outsized addition; its bold arena-

like circular courtyard now houses swifts,
whose nests were moved there deliberately
from the far more precious courtyards of the kaliphs.

And even when the Christians tried to copy
the Moors' artistry—the Alcazar in Seville—
they couldn't quite achieve the same sublimity

but settled for the purely ornamental.
Perhaps it's the lack of Arabic script,
their slight to Allah, the Great and the Merciful?

Or perhaps the Alcazar's just harder to co-opt
to *my* insatiable agenda,
at which I've—nonetheless—proved inept.

It's certainly not as if the Alhambra—
just look at it—is anything but impervious
to my designs on it (*It's time, Señora*).

But I, too, am willfully oblivious
of what was ordained here: at worst, genocide
at best, human dislocation, en masse.

Aren't I obliged to count the dead?
or, at the very least, the gross indignities?
Wasn't I *myself* forced to hide

my Sabbath candles, pull *my* mezuzahs
off *my* doorposts, hang ham above *my* door
at Passover, race through the exodus

at a sotto voce seder in *my* cellar?
Unless I just gave in and moved again,
loaded what I could carry on a boat to Tangier

and sold it in a market in Chefchaouen
or Meknes or Marrakech or Fez,
perhaps to the forebears of this very woman

snapping pictures, her hijab weirdly conspicuous
in a masterpiece of Islamic art.
Is she, too, uneasy in this place:

my one-time compatriot, my counterpart?
We're each still the Christians' infidel
according to the imam I met, robed in white

in Cordoba's mosque-turned-cathedral,
who told me if he prayed, he'd be arrested.
My daughter was reading Arabic from the wall,

the florid letters so curved and twisted
he took over—knew the words from memory—
pleased to find some non-Muslims interested,

to whom he could explain, tell his story.
He'd lived in the States, knew we were Jews—
and—at least when it came to our shared history

of Christian rulers—saw us as allies—
to which I say inshallah; if only
God would make this thought materialize

and not just according to the cynical cliché
(my enemies' enemies my friends)
but with some real chance of pertinacity,

though I'm not sure how you develop bonds
when the two participating parties
can't even agree on a split second's

history, much less a century's,
unless we go back half a millennium,
which, I'm gradually coming to realize,

is what I'm after here: that golden interim
of Muslim-Jewish serendipity
even if it *has* been exposed as sham.

Does it need to be true, if we agree?
Once upon a time in Al-Andalus
we reached a climax of civility

and cultural achievement: Muslims and Jews.
We have to start somewhere; why not myth?
What choice do we have? Just look at us.

Bloodbath after bloodbath after bloodbath.
Or don't look. Who can look at what we do?
Death. Revenge death. Revenge death. Death—

the *justice justice* we must *pursue*
collateral damage of inveterate war
slated to continue and continue.

Of course I retreat. I'll go anywhere,
believe anything, misconstrue
any bit of evidence if it might cleanse the air

of all this unforgiving residue
until it's safe again for human breath.
If I saw a way forward, I would go.

In the meantime, I'll withdraw into the monolith
they called *the Golden Age* in Hebrew school,
everyone we studied a polymath:

—this kaliph a poet, that rabbinical
scholar intimate with higher math,
this poet annotating Aristotle,

whose writings got to Latin via the oblique path
of Arabic translation from the Greek . . .
That part, at least, isn't myth—

even Hebrew poets wrote treatises in Arabic,
the universal language of higher thought.
But what I'm after is the acclaimed, idyllic

Jewish/Muslim partnership . . . *Not quite,*
says my friend (the expert), who knows.
Okay. So it's nonsense, I admit.

Still, look at this exquisite place. It glows.
I've returned again for the nighttime tour;
the patterns, in this semi-light, disclose

a rare affinity with the obscure,
a thousand pathways to a distant truth
which here feels unusually near.

If history founders, I'll escape to myth;
if myth collapses, I'll pair up each word
transfiguring each chiseled wall with faith

to one my own shepherds overheard;
and if that proves hopeless, there's still architecture,
its prophecies directly overhead.

But they're shooing us out. I can't stay here.
And I haven't begun to crack what's underneath,
its mysteries importunate but clear,

symmetry their double bind, their zenith,
their alibi, their fate, their metaphor . . .
each differential, though a hairsbreadth,

potentially, at least, oracular,
a grace note in a canticle connecting earth
to every other celestial sphere

or so surmised Pythagoras, who'd ordained math
discernible even to the ear.
If plucked strings of proportionate length

yield ideal harmonies, why not press further
and contemplate a music pinging forth
as moons and planets travel through the ether,

each on its taut, symmetric path?
I, for one, believe it's there,
that my seventeen symmetries of length and breadth

are part of it—their song that pure—
that they've just stopped a while to catch their breath.
Soon, they'll be singing in my ear.

ACKNOWLEDGMENTS

Grateful acknowledgment is made to the following publications, where the poems listed first appeared, sometimes under different titles: *Able Muse*, "Autumn Ghazal," "Backyard Meteor," "Spring Arrives Late to Salt Lake City," "The Stork in the Heavens, Revisited"; *Antioch Review*, "My Lookalike at the Krishna Temple," "Sonnet for My Backyard Crickets, Two Weeks Gone," "*Tilia cordata*"; *14Bytes*, "Storm Clouds over Lupines: Villanelle"; *Jewish Journal*, "Moonrise, Salt Lake City"; *Kenyon Review Online*, "Counting My Losses"; *Michigan Quarterly Review*, "Poems from the Alhambra"; *New Ohio Review*, "Fez Postcard/Call to Prayer"; *Southern Review*, "Winter Sonnet," "Psalm 27 on Newark AirTrain (mid-December, 4:15 p.m.)"; *Southwest Review*, "Autobiography with Joseph"; *Spillway*, "Autumn Ghazal."

Thanks to the University of Utah Research Committee for funding research in Darmstadt, Germany, and at the Alhambra, in Granada, Spain, and to the Taft-Nicholson Center at the University of Utah, where a number of these poems were begun.

I am grateful to Daniel Goroff, who first alerted me to the mathematical wonders of the Alhambra, and to Janine Parker and Paul Daniels, who patiently explained wallpaper symmetry to me. My gratitude, as always, to Wayne Koestenbaum and Barry Weller, for their invaluable attention to these poems.